Shadows and Silhouettes

Sharday Cage

Also by Sakura Publishing

When Heaven Calls

Lost Evidents

Did I Really Do My Hair for This? The Dating Disasters of a Not So Desperate Girl

Defeat Wheat: Your Guide to Eliminating Gluten and Losing Weight

Death of a Black Star

Elvolution

The Valley of Anchor

Joonie and the Great Harbinger Stampede

Because I'm Small Now and You Love Me: The World According to My Four-Year-Old

My Awfully Wedded Life

Without Boundaries

Praise for Sharday Cage

"Her poems are wise, edgy, funky, relevant, and universal. Best of all, to steal a phrase from the old jazzmen, her poems 'swing.' She has impeccable pace, rhythm, and timing. Sharday's poetry is a joy to read."—**Milo Samardzija, novelist and partner in the The Third City.org, a blog dedicated to new and irreverent writing**

"Sharday as an individual [is] an epitome of humanity, a global citizen in every shape and form. She is definitely an agent of change living in a junk, money-driven society…she is an ambassador for humanity and justice across the globe."—**Abraham Eddie "Master" Mkhatshwa, poet based in Durban, Kwa-Zulu Natal, South Africa**

Shadows and Silhouettes

Sharday Cage

SAKURA PUBLISHING
Hermitage, Pennsylvania
USA

Shadows and Silhouettes

Copyright © 2013 by Sharday Cage

All rights reserved. Published in the United States by Sakura Publishing in 2013. No part of this publication may be reproduced, distributed, or transmitted in any form or by any means, including photocopying, recording, or other electronic or mechanical methods, without the prior written permission of the publisher, except in the case of brief quotations embodied in critical reviews and certain other noncommercial uses permitted by copyright law. For permission requests, write to the publisher, addressed "Attention: Permissions Coordinator," at the address below.

Sakura Publishing
PO BOX 1681
Hermitage, PA 16148
www.sakura-publishing.com

Ordering Information:
Quantity sales. Special discounts are available on quantity purchases by corporations, associations, and others. For details, contact the publisher at the address above.

Orders by U.S. trade bookstores and wholesalers. Please contact Sakura Publishing: Tel: (330) 360-5131; or visit www.sakura-publishing.com.

Book Cover and Design by Desislav Iliev
Book Interior Editing and Design by Sarah Engdahl
Illustrations by Desislav Iliev
View more artwork by Desislav Iliev at www.dexvision.com

www.sakura-publishing.com

First Edition
Printed in the United States of America
ISBN-10: 0988962802
ISBN-13: 978-0-9889628-0-4
14 13 12 11 10 / 10 9 8 7 6 5 4 3 2 1

Sometimes I write all these words on paper and afterwards never really understand how I put it all there. I just assume I am God's worker pushing out the gift He gave to me. I feel very blessed to do this and even more blessed to share it with you. I would like to thank all my family and friends for their love and unconditional support; it truly means everything to me. Special thanks to Laverta Cage, William Visor, Wendy Richards, Gabriela Raudales-Richards, Derek Vasconi, Sarah Engdahl, and Desislav Iliev.

I think any true writer or poet has no absolute fear of truth, whether it is blinding with light or clouded in darkness. Whatever truth has decided to decorate itself in, we tell it without the slightest bit of corruption, even if it is ugly because a writer or poet can in any doubt still make it beautiful. I have a story just like anyone else and "Shadows & Silhouettes" is my story, where every word is a piece of my past or a representation of who I am. This collection of prose is my life, and I'm not ashamed or embarrassed of it as I once was somewhere in time. I'm growing and developing who I am as a writer and becoming comfortable in that skin, where truth is nothing to be frightened of—in fact, it is complete liberation. I wanted to share my freedom with you.

Table of Contents

Acknowledgements	i
Note from the Author	iii
Rebirth	1
The Day My Brother Died	3
Grave Talk	5
The Painful Things	6
Graffiti Mouth	8
Music	10
Lovers and Friends	11
Lover's Cup	12
Summer Solstice	13
Dirt	16
My Mother, the Queen	17
Touch	18
Glittering Cloud	20
Gone	21

T.B.D.	22
Alone	23
Naked	24
War Life	25
Sin	27
Choir Concerts and Drama Musicals	28
Shadows & Silhouettes	29
The Devil Inside	31
Sixth Grade History Class	32
Daddy	34
Mine	35
A.I.B.A. Pt. 1	36
Impossible Possibility	37
LOL	38
A.I.B.A. Pt. 2	39
My Mother, the Superhero	41
Runaway	43
Diamonds Are Forever	44

Poison	46
Dreams	47
Inevitable	49
Earth	50
Legs	51
Rejection	52
Writer	53
Hero	54
The Fall	55
Death	56
Chains	57
About the Author	61
About the Artist	63

Rebirth

There is hurt and then there is agony. One of course is gentler than the other and, more importantly, bearable. I can thoroughly explain the difference by the way it defines itself on my body. Hurt is a squint, a sour crash crusting along my candied skin, exploding with bitterness as I bleed out spoiled contents. Though it pours a temporary pain, the sting is poignant and memorable as sometimes its scars last forever. Agony is more of a harsh wind ripping against my flimsy skin, causing a ripple effect that is harshly cold, but ironically I feel as if I'm being burned alive. I am fire and ice when the severing of my limbs begins. When it cuts, it feels like hailing saw knives, hacking at me limb from limb, each a heavy blow until winter's bone, until all that's left of me is rusted cartilage and my gaping mouth full of maggots. But yay to the feast of flies, a praise of thanksgiving; though I was a result of your decadence, my death does not sleep in total vain. Seasons change and I am decomposing. Who will sprout seeds in me and birth forth a tree out of me? Let me be leaves and be at peace for once. A green thing in tune with the earth, in constant rhythm of the whispering winds. I will dance until the clock strikes ever. Forever never ends, nor will my hips relent or my legs consent to the stillness of sorrow. My hands have touched peace because I let you go. There is no time for crying because the music does not end. The sun is too busy sizzling, readying the record player while the air is cracking, trying to find the sound I can move to. Then the whistling starts as I sway and sway until I'm caught in forever. There is earth's perspective and there is tragedy's. You could say how tragically I died or in my resurrection how victoriously I lived. There is freedom and then there is eternity. I will dance forevermore.

The Day My Brother Died

The sun, dressed in its spoils of heat, will always rise and make a victory of it. One must be full of pride to never miss a dawn or full of duty to be crowned with such golden glory. The responsibility it must take to consistently rejuvenate a suffering people who count on its warmth to touch the coldest corners of their insides. A mission of infinite servitude, to set ablaze the inhumane, diagnosed with the foreign frozen. The kind of chill that makes the devil hot and the surrounding hell like molten lava. The sun, fired with certainty, will light us in troubled times giving us reason to open our eyes one more time. It will rise and it will fall, leaving an unending trail of beauty behind. Very few things I can depend on, but I can depend on that. If my brother was as dependable as the sun, maybe we would still be dancing among the sun's golden shards reflecting from the windows and into our eyes. Maybe the overabundance of laughter would still be mounded on the walls of our house, and you would have to peel the layers of joy to find the sorrow buried beneath. Maybe I wouldn't have to hold this leather whip and take it to my backside as a form of repentance for the sins unexplained or unaccounted for. I ask God to look at each wound, bloodied and torn, as a form of apologies, maybe for crimes from generations past to undo generational curses or future lies which birth this live death. My brother, like Lazarus declined, however resurrected by some other. The moment he spoke, I knew he was gone, like a walking glitch or grey fuzz on the television screen. He was disconnected, permanently faded into lost signals. I hid behind my door, behind the reality of non-existent superheroes and villains that had nothing to do with a resolution or happy ending. This was hiding; this was living with it. My brother is a pill popper, a mute, a vessel of his former self. I cannot linger on the cruelty of fate because it is only air dancing around decisions. Ultimately we pick one of them never knowing its truth or consequences. Our humanness proposes we dance around should've, could've, would've, a music so horrid that it is no longer a dance but a continual run that leads to endless questioning. I am afraid the only answers are but broken particles found on the ground in search for the one that doesn't exist. No destination, just constantly we run. All I can do is depend on the sun. It is faithful and it warms those cold corners that want to freeze. As long as the sun rises, I will be okay.

Grave Talk

Lavished in a ghoul's gown, I've lain with the unrest, making awkward conversation over a cup of dirty rain. We chatter about what could have been as insects hush us quiet from the underground walls. There is no love secured for the labored ant—just unrequited passion to create channels, endless channels. But our words surpass authority, rising above the ground into a wind of echoes. They travel everywhere until there is a kindred ear mistaking ours for God's, and oh how they listen with a sharp ear and shaky knees. There is a certain kind of talk spoken by the dead that is only reserved for the living in order to repair the broken things that lie haphazard on the floor. Pick it up and be moved from the stagnant objects that are but premeditated injuries. Be part of the wounded or walk over it with every passing and wounded still. You pray it will be there when you come back so you can glare once more. From your chair you stare indigenously or stand stuck between the corners of a complacent room. The darkness is a haunted house and its mouth the creaky doors that swallow you into a poltergeist lair. I have very little patience for supernatural wishes! I must act on my purpose as I am still in existence.

The Painful Things

My mother and father were disappointing together but, separately, they had their moments. From what I gather of the two, they loved peacefully for a time but loved paranoia for a time longer. I see traces of another ending, but they are immediately brushed away like wavering hands in cigarette smoke. Jealousy is a quiet serial killer sitting in an unlit car, watching your every move from the darkness of a New York City neighborhood. Black-rimmed glasses with a thick lens, watching motionless with a sadistic patience, waiting for the perfect scenario. The moment you fear what is not there is when the bushes rustle and the signs squeak and the wind whistles. Footsteps moved by uncertainty, and that is when jealously strikes, with snakelike precision in the heat of doubt. My parents' truth is somewhere buried by the graves of their dear mothers, my grandmothers. I was closer to my mother's mother; she lived longer, but she was dead living, which was unfair. But even in her defects I'd rather have the broken her opposed to not having her at all. My dad fades in and out of how she used to be before schizophrenia, and I wonder how that woman lived. I tried to jump into his memory while it was still moving to take a look behind the sheer white curtains of a woman who was still untarnished. She still seemed too far away to see, let alone know. My dad's mother, I couldn't describe to you her features, but I have one strong memory of her making me a white turtle neck with cherries on it. But her face is always blurry. For a while I wondered if I only created that memory just so I had something of her, but my father likes to remind me she loved to hold me, so I call it truth because you make things for people you love. I was very young when she died. My father's side of the family has always remained a bit of a rumor to me, while his old childhood home flashes in and out of my consciousness like a ghost house. I'm often daunted by the vagueness of sudden occasional moments that flicker on and off across my mind, vanishing into untraceable scenes, like I dreamt it. My fingers graze the antique piano keys. The countless pictures in black and white or a dying toasted burnt orange color, old and faded on the wall filled with people I would never know. The smell of fried bologna in the kitchen, which my dad would make every time we visited him. The door to the backyard was a gateway. The moment I opened the screen door, the overabundance of light would swallow my breath and release my imagination to these creature-esque statues and fountains, which drifted me into some sort of fairytale. I would stand there for a long time wondering if my dad would ever find me out here. I always walked to the edge of the hill, though when I was little it was more like a cliff wondering if I was in heaven. I remember one room of the house; it was the scariest. It was the room my father's mother was dying in. She laid there in a stretcher for most of my young childhood. My father would tell me to go in there to give her a hug. It felt like the kind of journey I was too young for. There was no laughter where she was, just a long hallway stretching its limits to a silent room where her breathe was still and her heart was tired. This was a lot like my parents.

Graffiti Mouth

You had yellow-stained lies painted on your teeth. Your tongue slithered and your saliva gathered, forming a gang of corrupters to graffiti my name into the four walls of your mouth. You built the destruction before the construction, craving the ruins much like archaeologists do, preserving the pain to display it as beauty. The stench coming from your mouth was as foul as the remnants of last night's dinner, cigarette smoke, and shots of tequila. I would watch you talk waiting for your breath to swim to my nose. I was searching for truth but I should've known you would filter your words through Crest mouthwash to hide your iniquities. I imagine your mouth being caked with dust and spite, bound to deteriorate any ounce of decency you had left. Humanity is the scent of snow and the sight of the suns rising but you forgot about purity a long time ago. So when your talk smelled of ice and everglades, I believed you. The existence of lies is not much older than the earth's so its odor is similar to death. It never bathes or clothes itself in clean laundry. Lies never smell fresh, and somewhere I know there was a sink that had to swallow the truth less putrid you spit into it. Your sentences were framed with the kind of pictures you see at Wal-Mart: perfect. With a breath like that, you would think it would take more than a pocket of change to be what you are not. I wish I could just break your jaw and be done with it. Take one last look at the jagged bones that could grind such sweet songs into heavy metal music that pierced my ears repeatedly. You look for my pain like balloons in the air or confetti on the floor—to claim some sort of victory as the wax bleeds from birthday candles that still burn. After all this time you gaze at me with a love of war and your passion for revenge remains unhinged. I fear you will die with a soldier's heart. You will see bombs like fireworks and forgiveness through bitterness. You will suffer at the sun's sunsets like the conclusion of an explosion, sitting perplexed on the edge of a mountain, wondering if love ever existed.

Music

If God is our authority, though righteously, and the devil, the anarchist, then man in his democratic splendor gave birth to music: an ode to the two. Like any child adorned in smooth flesh that becomes suddenly corrupted by the wild and rough hairs of puberty, there grows a rapid defiance or need of expression or simply the need to be heard. To feel, celebrate, defy, and obey. The sound gave room for breath, a dwelling place to be free in this instant of be. To exist in a moment and the feeling it exhaled out, unmotivated by good or evil but by instinct, whether that be for good or for evil. Music became the mass recording of a people's bible written by the blood of life of those who shed for it. I am a child of music, headphone placenta and all. Even my name was a birthright to the right side of the throne of song. In the womb it gave me breath simply in preparation for a world that was breathtaking.

Lovers and Friends

If left alone for too long, there is no friendship between you and me, just two lovers breathing behind a pained silence, clinging ferociously to a word that will somehow bind our permanence: "friends." And though it may be an inconvenient pleasure, we still are. Eventually the darkness times its little black watch to our exact fate, the motioning of our hands searching for one another, the disparity of our unsucked lips. We are finding our way back to a resolution that refuses to be claimed by either one of us for fear has robbed us of many words, so we act our passion through a silent monologue recited by our lips. And still after the violent urgency of pulling and squeezing, biting and grabbing, we force a climactic enlightenment, almost simultaneously dimming as quickly as it lit, trying to understand what we do not understand. You always find an excuse for our unthinkable outburst. "I don't know what happened." I blame myself for your suddenness to assume our impossibility, because for a time I believed it impossible, too.

Lover's Cup

Waking up for the first time after your kiss was hangover's bliss. No pain, though heavily induced with a drunken air. My eyes were filmed with milky dew as I roamed the night and found nothing but a linear blur. I put my head in my hands rubbing for sobriety as everything else kept me stuck in place. I wanted to stand but I was caught in the high. It wasn't until the pull of your hands that would finally move me. Your fierce subtlety to grab me so roughly yet kiss me so softly intoxicated my limbs that suddenly fell limp. As your hands traced my frame one last time, I propped my head on the shelter of your shoulders and hovering over my eyes, the infinite sky. It all felt too uncommonly close, like I could lasso the moon to you or pluck a star for you. As you opened my car door, I fell back in like it was made of sea, floating recklessly, waiting for you to jump back in, but quickly you shut my door and waved me off. I passed the police officer who was surveying the area all night long, the one who may have passed a couple times before while my face was on yours; I was busy drinking from my lover's lips. He simply smiled at me and I smiled back and though my eyes were lazy and sloppy, he didn't bother pulling me over. He must have known I was drunk from my lover's cup.

Summer Solstice

The summer's beauty provided no solace to me as I sat alone in the living room one hot afternoon. I could see the silhouette of summer behind the white curtain and the sun was still smiling, the trees still waving, and the cicadas were still singing. So much joy I thought. Does the summer know how to turn away from the celebration and sympathize with the mourners for once? I needed the thunder to pound, the dark grey clouds to roll in, and for the lightning to flash. I needed sufferers, for nature's ugly side to awaken the darkened gloom. I needed someone else to be as angry as I was. I needed the rain to cry because I was scared, too. I needed the night to come for me so I could feel like I wasn't dark alone. I could feel the pain churning in my stomach like poison figuring its way out. I was never a child to act hasty because life really had never been that cruel to me, probably because it never really noticed me either. But on the last summer's day, life picked me out of the crowd, a crowd of billions, and I wonder if I looked like a lost child holding a single red balloon. When it found me, my pain was an utter delight, a brunch or a midday snack, but it was watching my life spiral into a beautiful cacophony, music to life's ears. My anger had risen to a boiling point and I could feel my head throbbing as my thoughts hammered away into opposite sides of my head. I placed two fingers from each of my hands and pressed them gently against the indentation above my sideburns where the pulsating veins were protruding out of my skin. For the first time in my life I was not okay. I was not going to be able to defuse the bomb that was counting down in my system, and it was the first time I didn't want to. I did not seek God in that moment, but it doesn't mean He wasn't there watching me with sad eyes. I wanted no one there but Him, though I couldn't bring myself to talk to Him as I'm sure He felt my animosity toward Him for things He did not do or control, but He knew I knew that, too. He was my everything as I felt Him all over me, but equally my nothing because I still couldn't see Him.

I resented that because I was young and immature in wisdom, in need of physicality. I thought about my mother and the wars we fought. We were titans, mighty and strong, unwilling to end until our hearts' last beats. With missing limbs, bloody tears, and broken bones we fought through her depression, my rebellion, her lack of sentiment, my feelings of being unloved. I thought about my grandmother, a schizophrenic, who we were shipping to a nursery home. We might as well send her in a coffin because it was just a waiting room for the dead, I thought. I remember being so angry with my mother, but I was young and immature in wisdom. How can the sick take care of the sick? Yet my mother did it for so long that I had no choice but to believe she was somehow built for it. But even the mightiest inventions break over time and the brokenness filled her eyes like a forsaken river. I started to massage the areas in my head where I was beginning to feel the cracks show, but it was too late. I thought about my brother now, who was diagnosed with the same sickness as my grandmother. I was trying to come to terms with this troubling going around on my insides and whether it was of great importance pertaining to my sanity. Should I let this up or keep it down? I am completely uncertain of the explosions in my chest, but I could feel pieces of me that were blown to smithereens because of what happened to my brother, and I have the utmost fear that I was beyond repair. My head was aching the way it did when I was young. I would get the most mind-breaking headaches and the only medicine that would suffice was my own haunting screams that would ricochet off the walls, echoing like tortured souls until I passed out. I would wake up from a long sleep as if magic had cured me, but I was no longer a child and screaming would not cure me. I knew the cure: college. It was my escape route, the only exit I knew of to flee from the flames. I will die if I stay here, I thought. I have no money and my parents have no money, but I am not ready to die. I felt the house crumbling above me and the rocks that were crashing onto me. My family, my home, and the town I lived in my whole life were foreign to me, a stranger in a black trench coat holding a pillow over my face, suffocating me with an expressionless trance, irritatingly waiting for me to die. Except I would not. I was still young and strong, but I finally gave into the pain. I let it bleed and I let it pour forth. On that last summer's day, I screamed, I howled, I cried, I threw what I could, I punched, I kicked, I lay on the floor writhing in terror. I was fighting my own self war. I was losing my childhood and the innocence it stood for. I was finding the harsh unapologetic realities of life. I was growing up.

Dirt

I have been vulgar with my tongue. I have licked the crevices of dirty corners searching for the grime no one else would taste—the kind that could be found beneath the dining room table where gluttons and scavengers feast. I wanted to prepare you for the meals you were unprepared to eat, set the placements of silverware you couldn't place. I wanted to show you the difference between dining and ravaging because it is easy to call one the other if not both are defined. I did this so that you might have a chance at breath, because one must know death in order to know life. I must speak on the ills as well as the good for you to know ultimate truth, every truth, damned or divine.

My Mother, the Queen

My mother and her infinite wealth of golden screams hidden within a box in her diaphragm that remained slightly opened at all times. It did not take much before the haunting began, loosed to our reality, an echo of violence. For a time, there was no peace resting inside her darkness, just heavy breathing and a pair of hunter's eyes flickering with an aggressive anticipation. Even the most peaceful person could no longer contain a harmonious composure when her sudden lashings of noise ripped through your earlobe, ringing violently like bells wrapped around knifes. She used them to write her name on your serenity, and as the blood spilled out from your extremities so did your self-control and effortless poise. My mother had a queen's tongue: demanding and rebellious, powerful and uncensored, and mostly unfathomed by man and his authoritative instinct to bring her to her knees. With her head raised high and elongated neck, she would only lower her eyes to look down on you. She would never forfeit her power to a man and so silently she pledged a life of loneliness in order to sustain her throne. There were times I felt a sense of sympathy for her, until I realized this fate may be my own.

Touch

For a moment, within the galaxy of your pupil, I caught a glimpse of your humanity. It glazed over your eyes like silky foam pleading its last moments of existence to me. Your lips, coded with inscriptions, unraveled a burden to me in the form of a kiss. Wandering in the feeling, a mixture of pain and pleasure rested on my skin, seeping into my lifeless pores, transcending that paralyzing part of me when my reality was untouched. I was taken past time where time never defines itself in alternate worlds, never really landing, just in constant cosmic floating. However, my ignorance, an overcrowded party chattering about proximity and anticipation, all the while your skin is decaying. I lack certain discernment in the night hour but there have been premonitions of such unions between you and I that I envisioned since the moment you left. It's always easy to see the inevitable but quite difficult to interpret the unsettled soul. But your silence was the true reckoning, killing off any part of you that understood I was never against you. Your eerie nothingness moved me like a heavy wave into the rocky edges. We were describing who we were together now: two drowning strangers reaching out to a past that no longer claimed us, and we couldn't fully claim it either. It was days after you left that it occurred to me you weren't planning on coming back. There was something I was supposed to do or say to you and I didn't because I was only thinking about myself again. I cannot save you. Either I am your death or you want me dead. Swallowed by the sea, I made peace in the belly of the whale, waiting for the kind of death between you and I that would set you free.

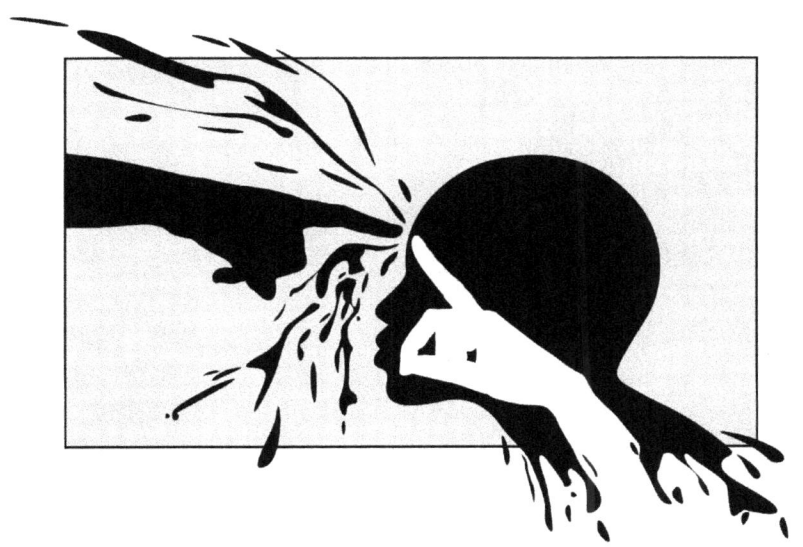

Glittering Cloud

I watch the becoming world from a cloud while I am. I don't fear the vacant expanse. I am busy in awe of the slow motioning, the slight romanticism of the detailed still, and the passion of the quiet forming. There is the lightning's boom thundering a god's roar. The pounding grabs hold of my heart and beats a drumming song that only the ancestors of the first natives can hear. They chant within the rhythm of the rain. As rain cries, the air mixes with its tears, leaving a scent behind from making love that turned into perfume. A gift for the sea and still adorned as it shimmers a light of thanksgiving. The sky, no longer ruled by night or day or sun or moon but forever a midnight blue skin tone with a grey blush and a heavy glow. Emanating from the shadows of what is were the foundations of what was. Born again into a new existence where light and darkness stand still, never again to conquer but bleed each other to life in a cosmic fire of sapphire. I would blatantly deny any wealth or land, any crown or rule for this deserted beauty. I saw it once beneath a glittering cloud while it was still becoming like you. It was behind the shadowed mountains of South Africa, quietly waiting to fade in and out of time. My eyes were stuck in the dim brightness as we drove past. I wanted to jump out of the car and follow what those mountains had left us for a long time ago. That image was worth the running away but it would only disappear if I didn't create it forevermore. Now I am, resting in this cloud of fragile churning where I took a temporary sky and made it law. And I, the hieroglyphics to the unyielding, will sit on the throne of heaven's passion watching the becoming world hate then love, hate again then love again, each time more brutally and beautifully than before.

Gone

I am ready to be pulled by some spiritual air weaving tales of hopefulness, or swayed by a gust of miraculous wind to ignite a powerful movement, leaving the land abandoned and deserted. Mutiny in the form of a disappearing breed, in protest of the sweltering heat one would melt in. When they come for you and me, let us be long gone from the kitchen chair with unlocked chains and emptied ropes. Let fire burn fire. But when the cool voices find our particular ear, let us heed that call. Fear was no longer the last option; the graves from the graveyards are. Let us become what they are not. Let us finish the unfinished.

T.B.D.

How can I not be moved if not by time? By you then, within the ticking of your subtle words slowly transitioning themselves into hidden sentiment. Once cold hard letters, stiff at the touch, unable to shift or transform, but resting there in constant silence of unimportant meaning. What changed then? Within the secrecy of empty black spaces, I mean? Before, you were just a friendly wanderer passing by on rare occasion with only a hello, goodbye, and a handful of mischievous banter to your name, and then slowly kindling these honeyed words, suggesting we could evolve from barely eating to a table of splendor where our talk would be full of salty and sweet delights. I find your uncertainty intriguing and, even more, the silence you've taken on to address your fondness for me. Now this story I could read more of and of course the conclusion of this book I would be open to resolve.

Alone

I stand alone. This seems to be the me I really am. In the middle of swaying weeds that wave for my undivided attention, I just stare past them waiting to be moved. On top of some prestigious mountain that presides over the land below it while I sit on its lap, anticipating a kingdom's capture. Stranded along the desert plains, buried beneath Christmas snow, the music of children laughing and light rain warming my solitude like a soft blanket. I sit on the edge of my bed and there is no one there but me. Head resting on knee, arms wrapped around legs, afraid to leave. This is my head, though my reality has dreamed up a slightly different tale. I've built this crowded world that is decorated with people. It is filled with animated memories and wild-like faces, but after the clapping seals, the obedient lion, and the ballerina elephant, it is just me in sequins dancing on air. After the show, just my tightrope and barren lair.

Naked

I've been obscene for days, twisted up in my own nakedness, appearing loose and sinful before the darkness as it spills over me. I sit cracked and proud as my limbs remain out of place, bending with a contorted properness, unwilling to mend my brokenness. I shatter into a complete picture hanging on to broken bones, like a perfect breakable piece. With desperation I bleed like an overthrown queen, spewing out blood without batting an eyelash or giving into an ounce of anguish. I am a timeless victim with eyes wide open. I had no fear of death when it came for me because I was waiting for you. I watched death kill me slowly and still, though lifeless, I wait for you. Haunted and unwilling, I remain an echo, a distant ghost. A hundred moans that sound the same, coded in screams like murdered murmurs. I choke from my own blood babbling its rustic wine, swallowing drops of bitter blindness to stay immortal waiting for you. Pleading my last moments of light like a second of hope straining...I'm waiting for you. I'm waiting for you to save me from my own self-shame that I exist in mere ruins, but I want you to look at me with eyes similar to God's. Proclaim me not damaged but adorn me in pearls and declare me still beautifully born as I die so that I could prove love did not.

War Life

This very room is shrinking despite me. Maybe *to* spite me, I suppose. I refuse to shrivel into a tiny ball and roll into one of its dark corners waiting to die. There are obstacles that anticipate this kind of demise, and I hear them laughing outside my window, a distant disturbance reminiscent of circus clowns. I must admit, I am toppling and stumbling over the rushing objects projecting themselves at me. Their faces glare at me with retribution. A candlestick burns its wick as it flings toward me, but what had I done to receive such hatred? Four walls have unexpectedly closed in with insensitive passion, leaving me awestruck as I stand stuck in the instant. I feel this flood of depression cleanse over me and my odor is the stench I've often smelled at gravesites and nursing homes. Melted soap and perfume bottles have already made sacrifices of themselves against the wooden floor in faith to darker powers I do not yet understand. Where is my God in all of this? Does He know what the devil has done to me? But I feel Him there and I think He's waiting for me to do something, but I don't know what to do. My first instinct, the instinct of any living creature, is to survive, which meant rushing to the door and leaving all this behind. I don't even know where to begin to combat the forces that exceed my strength. For if I speak, they would take away my sound, and if I fought them with my limbs, they would break them. The doors are locked and the windows are jammed. Should I give up my life? I am stagnant in a moment that has no compassion for me. I am in constant pursuit of nothingness and my progression is useless. Then I think of God again. If I run, what shall come of it? Surely God created them for such but the mind was his ultimate gift. And the result to my endlessness would lead to what? The woods where I would then watch the trees turn against me? Our surroundings are in constant contrast to our existence. In utter uproar of our permanent being, warring at our souls until we give out and die like we never lived at all. I think I realize that God is not waiting for to me run, He's not waiting for me to figure a way out, and He's not up there trying to make a way for me to escape. He is waiting for me to stand in the middle of this room and take the hell brought upon me. With my back laid up against the wall, I finally walk towards the center of the room and I endure. I am enduring. Though amidst this suffering, I try not to complain or give into its pain, and ultimately I know this pleases God. So I will continue on with an armored heart, inside still soft and sweet liquidized love, and bear with my own hands this war life, until it crashes onto me, leaving me standing tall, looking at the rubble it's left behind as a reminder that it did not win my soul.

Sin

I've repressed the sins I regret the most. Shame has found me now and made me over, drooping one side of my face so that I look melted and wicked and then turning out my bones to distort my body as a sign of un-forgiveness. I'm forced into seclusion as it chained me to its immortal shadows, coasting me into some skyscraper cave centered within dusted mountains rocked with punishable pasts. I live among sins, kidnapped though abiding, giving into their torturous rule. I was part of the damned, destined to be pitied and slaved, dwelling among the corrupted, mounted in the mountains that shined their misery over sleepwalkers. During the night, when the whispers rode out to find the memories I denied, I could peacefully, for a time, listen to the echoes from the drops of water that would amuse me with a song. There was a pool of water I was forced to drink from. It did not reveal my own silhouette, but instead a collage of moments forgotten that were thought to be in the hands of God. I watch with a distant familiarity, occasionally touching the water and tasting the moment with my tongue to make sure it was real. My sins envelope me and I'm forever indebted. I open my mouth and hidden inside the corner of my right cheek are the prettiest rocks I could find. I was filled with filth from head to toe but I offered the rocks as a form of repayment. I wanted to prove, as dirty as I am, that I could in fact still offer something clean. There was a silence that had overtaken the cave as if time had muted and for a minute, I thought, they were marveling at me. After the silence had ended, my gift was unaccepted. The voices told me they had no control over my being there and that it was only I who could control that.

Choir Concerts and Drama Musicals

I had a name but it left me when I stood on stage. I could see faded faces in the crowd but they all too remained nameless. I remember most that there was no one there to call me by my name, to help me remember who I was. I let the light blind me and the darkness hide them. If you look closely, I was the girl singing to no one. My eyes wandered back and forth, gazing at the parents who were gazing at their children. Occasionally, my eyes would find one of my teachers. I would smile and remember they knew my name. I was always looking for the boy I loved, hoping he would call out and call me by my name. I was always hopeful, praying it wasn't too late for someone to yell and scream unremorsefully, that there was someone out there with a bouquet of roses and my name. When the stage lights turned off and the auditorium lights turned on, we smiled victoriously like we survived some sort of epic battle, as we were always celebrated with a standing ovation and a thunderous applause. I skim the crowd like an interesting book, quickly bouncing my eyes from wall to wall until they were straining with pain. I could feel my throat swell up as the realization sunk in: I was alone. There could be no one to claim the nameless. I would have to suffice with the applauded scraps and whistled leftovers that no one owned, the noise that belonged to everyone. I reached out for what I could to keep myself from crying.

Shadows & Silhouettes

I've built such a fond connection to the silent seas or any endless empty. I stare passionately at the blushing sunset flirting with the approaching night and its starry eyes that return to me with such light. I roam infinite greens: apple greens, olive greens, forest green weeds—they all dance for me. There is no shadow I cannot find or any silhouette I cannot outline. You could define me to an extent by this imperial beauty, this overwhelming divine that stretches throughout the quiet corners of the earth. It is never demanding or pleading for attention to be admired or adorned; it just is. Perhaps appreciated by a random wanderer with an exact eye who could find solace in the seclusion. One who could relate to the drama of nothingness, the impact of the quiet, or the story of an unmoving picture and become part of what's always been. To be drawn within certainty's image, to seek out peace that is often only found through an honest God's work. Through the creation of God's holy hands is serenity truly discovered. Maybe it's the seen work of an unseen God that comforts me so because I can see what I am not supposed to. I can see God.

The Devil Inside

I hate the unsettling, disturbing images that taunt the mind like a quick slideshow of the devil's photography. Flickering random moments or still shots of actions better uncommitted or seen less before. Presenting disruptive pictures before the brain that blossomed out of possibility or sheer boredom. Every horror movie gives an ode to them as a worshiper to the unkind. The unwanted lurks like a crypt keeper giving off an overwhelming feeling that the devil is gnawing its way inside.

Sixth Grade History Class

I was so afraid they would figure me out, but they were still angels uncorrupted by the distortion of reality. They were levitating on purity, the last drops of heaven adults somehow could not see. I was afraid if they touched me, I would melt into the shadows, cozying up with the dark truth I belonged in, unaccepted by a white society and ostracized as a thing to be feared. No one took much notice of me until we were old enough to have our parents suck the innocence from the crevices of our brains. Life is already predestined to be judgmental as we roam here in various shapes and colors. Eventually it plays tug of war with us and God, sometimes banishing the perfect thoughts God once gave us as a birthright, replacing them with the ones ravaged by Life that come from centuries of perversion. The older you get, the more Life takes a toll on you. I started to see the thoughts of the young mirror the thoughts of the old, an undying reflection of destructive thinking. Even I had fallen victim to it. I would sit in class damp from sweat, watching the time tick uncaringly, or unknowingly maybe, knowing that my very year depended on at least one black student to come sit in class with me. I felt alone if they didn't.

At first, I hated watching the Civil Rights Movement in our history classes. I would cringe, grinding my teeth until the shards of bone rested beneath me like pencil shavings. I watched the teacher walk toward the VCR and my initial reaction, the one I cleverly reenacted in my head first, snatched the video cassette out of her hand viciously, growling with pain, "Do you understand what this could do to me!?" If no one had known a difference between them and I, than they would know now. The video symbolized the end to my blending in, to my sameness, to my being just like them. It was hard to swallow. I watched the policemen hose down black bodies. Young, old, women, and men, I kept swallowing. I tried to convince my mind to focus on my difficulty of swallowing in effort to distract my tears. I couldn't bring myself to look at anyone for fear of witnessing some 20 fair-skinned blue-eyed blonde-haired heads looking at me with wide accusatory eyes. They all looked the same through a blurry lens while the same lens magnified my absolute difference in perfect clarity. I was frozen into the historical screen in determination to be void of my actuality. I had never felt such huge waves of conflicting emotions before. I was filled with anger and love, guilt and embarrassment, passion and pain. Who were these people I was unequivocally bound to? Was it our color that connected us, or that it could've been me where they were? Only time bettered my fate, but they were responsible, too. From the pit of my stomach to the clenching of my teeth was a barbaric battle brewing inside me. Immediately nothing looked the same. I was handed this truth I didn't ask for, that I didn't want to know but there it was, sitting inconveniently in my hands corroded with dirt and filth. There was a monster waiting to be awakened and set free. I raised my eyes with a protective glare, cave-like, searching for a face that would create a war. If anyone said anything with the slightest offense, I was going to transform, my mouth widening to the size of my head and unleashing the souls I swallowed from the television screen. I would tear them all apart.

Daddy

I was a Daddy's girl without the daddy. At times, a figment of my imagination that occasionally materialized into existence, though it was never exactly the same. He was perfectly present in my dreams, watching me with constant adoration, throwing me on his shoulders, walking and holding hands with me through the park, but, in my reality, he was more like a weekend, a frying pan inflamed with onions and vegetables, a loving stranger, who often surrounded me with lovable unfamiliars. He reminded me of a ghost; he came and went, he was here then gone. I would find myself reaching out for his outline that was left from last week. I could no longer keep track of his frequencies, his tolerable inconsistencies. The times he never showed, I could see my reflection through my mother's eyes. I would perch my lips out, a ledge my tears could commit suicide on, and kick my legs back and forth as I sat on the couch with a feeling of abandonment. I was kicking the sand from my desert.

Mine

In a world that is barely mine. Literally, I cannot find a thing to my name, but he told me his lips were mine. Shyly, though with much greed, I happily accepted, scrapping and snatching his softly sweet words puckered inside his supple sweet lips. I stuffed my pockets until they were completely full and then the world, taking on a new appearance, was no longer unbearable but completely filled up. Because his lips and his words were everything to me, and suddenly the world was entirely mine.

A.I.B.A. Pt. 1

More than ever, my awkwardness takes precedence as I have nothing to say in a group of three who seem to have nothing to say to me. Finding a seat on the wooden floor, I converse amongst the stranger shadows to pass the time. I look at myself with a pleasing eye because I'm wearing a dress again, but no one else seems to care except the mystery that is always fond of the woman I've become. With a shiny red cup in my hand, I delighted in discussing my shadows from long ages past, and strangely enough they knew them, too. They tell me about my shadows that lurk from the closet doors, staring at me from across the room, praying they'll catch me in my demise. I fill the room with my invisibility as I enthrall myself in the movement of other peoples' shadows, moving alongside them as if they're talking to me. As lonely as I am, roasting slowly in the social solitude, I am afforded a grace by God: that man again who stops time and still looks at me like it's the very first time. It's a wonder he can see me as faded as I look, but his stare is so poignant, like he's looking at a thousand of me. I realize I love him, especially for these sweet simplicities, which is why when I kiss him, I consume him.

Impossible Possibility

I had to become self-aware; I forced it down like a side of green peas, scraping my fork back and forth, and then licking it clean afterwards. I refuse to walk around clueless, holding on to the hands of my vices, smiling and laughing like we're all friends as they happily pull me into coffee shops, reminiscing about my obliviousness. I know that skeletal, veiny creature known as paranoia plays a heavy role in my consciousness, too, crawling inside the creases of my brain, making a home like an extremist neighbor, whispering my flaws like corruptions, turning me into a suspicious overanalyzing freak. Luckily, I know the difference between the two. Paranoia is not my friend but an unstable ally. I remember in college, we were asked to list our best and worst characteristics and both were pretty easy. Even the bad ones, which I listed as: bad listener, short attention span, loud, hyper, financially inept, forgetful, gluttonous, procrastinator, time management and organizational issues. Everyone looked at me with bewilderment. I may have been the only one who listed just as many bad characteristics as good, and I was proud of that because I don't look at perfection like a hat resting at the edge of the bed that I may or may not wear before I walk out of the door. Perfection is the westward sun you hope to touch if you walk long enough, despite the limitless hills and the infinite valleys. Perfection is the last of the earth where land and sea abruptly end. Perfection is the impossible possibility. Perfection can never be achieved, but the glory is our efforts to always try to achieve it because the achieving never ends.

LOL

There is nothing funny about the nonexistent laugh. The laugh buried in silence—the chuckling, cackling, giggling quiet resounding from my closed coffin mouth. Behind the prison of my teeth is black awkwardness or words unknown. The ability to void out all inappropriateness or aid voiceless breath that has been mysteriously filled by the LOL. I am almost never laughing, but I send out constant reassurances that I am. Possibly, equally matched in kindness and fakeness, LOL is a generation's avoidance of conflict and verbal interaction, and its complete laziness to deal with the proper reply that one would actually give: an honest answer.

A.I.B.A. Pt. 2

Don't ask me if this prose is about you. I loved you from the moment I saw you, which is why I surrendered to the intricate wirings in my brain that had to be near you. They sparked and shot out in destruction when I denied the power you brought to me. I could've rioted in protest, initially pretending like I didn't see you, but the death I would have brought upon myself if I lied to my own truth—my legs never had a chance. I was afraid of who I would become if I walked away. Immediately my pride was shutdown and you moved me like you were the source of me. I walked without wanting and moved without choosing because the air was in alliance to gravity, who has only wanted nothing except to bring together anything that is love. The beginning was easy; fate was literally explaining our captivation for one another in the way we locked eyes and how they threw hooks into each other, hiking into the depth of our restricted caves, only to resurface with portions of our soul that were filled with the same substances. Unknowingly intertwined, our instincts knew before our minds, and somehow we had to put it together that we were born to find one another. But that kind of thing is not approached without consequence. Imagine the potency of that love and then add equally the hurt if the love is not handled correctly, whether it is misplaced, misunderstood, or not ready. You and I created a history of complexities and I have no intentions to tell the tall tale, especially when there is no happily ever after. Just after. We exist and our contentment sautés in the silence and the low sound of sizzling is our frustration that we are truly not satisfied. But we make the best of it because fear, if our love is great enough, is the one bitter manipulator to make us believe it was never meant to be.

My Mother, the Superhero

My mother comes off a little immortal. Her strength gathers in a circular bright light that seems to combust, creating a sense of stability in a chaotic world. She was a single parent but she had superpowers, I think. I remember being hungry but I never starved. As a child of the 90's, I was converted by McDonalds and other fast food chains to what good food is supposed to look like. The commercials teased us the worst—the slow pan across the burger, various angled shots giving off this larger than life appearance. That's what we wanted to eat every night as we salivated on ourselves, pleading and crying to her. My mother put my brother, cousins, and I to the test when we cried about necessity of the finer things, which to her translated to the wasteful things. "There's food in the cabinet!" she always said as she jetted off. "If you don't want to eat what's in there, you must not be hungry," she said as she flew in and out of the house constantly like lightning. One minute her voice shot across the room and the next she was gone. At times when I thought I was talking to her, instead I was only talking to the flustered wind she left behind. We searched and rummaged for the "food" she was talking about and would only find canned foods and ramen noodles. When food appeared really scarce, we got creative. Our favorite was butter and bread sandwiches. My childhood was a mixture of seasons; sometimes we lived with simple indulgences and other times the bare minimum, but our environment was never less than stable. I lived in the same quiet house in the same quiet neighborhood planted in the middle of our same quiet town for 18 years. Summer and its bright negativity would beam its high light directly beneath us at times when we had no AC to protect ourselves, but luckily the wooden floors were permanently refrigerated. I would come home from school, raise my shirt up, and lay in the coolness. When winter came, our home didn't always hug us with heat either, but we bundled up like little burritos until we found the warmness we were looking for.

The point is, we had rough times like most middle class families, but we could always make do with what was thrown at us mostly because of my mother and her instinctive ability to provide and maintain through any circumstance. There were times I knew she was leaving into the night to fight ambitious battles. There were probably swords and bullets involved and much bloodshed, so when I heard the door open late every night, I knew she'd won again. Sometimes there would even be a new Barbie doll in it for me, too. She took care of her mother and her two kids and somehow kept a sense of safety and security. I look back on it in wonderment, the resilience of a woman and the inability to fold under such pressure. If my mother wasn't a superhero, her ancestors were because that blood certainly flowed inside her veins. She had moments where her humanness showed, so maybe she was a hybrid: half hero, half human. Her emotions would rise up mostly in the form of anger and lash out at anyone who crossed her path. Sometimes, the biggest battles she fought were within her and I fear many of those battles she lost, succumbing to the fury building inside her from doing it all alone. But we all need weapons to combat against this life, and though I never agreed with her weapon of choice, she could survive with what she had. My brother and cousins knew to be quiet when my mother was angry, but it was extremely hard for me to deal with that rage part of her. I was the back-talker, the one who couldn't swallow her words into the black abyss of the forgotten. My stomach turned with every lashing she spoke at us, and maybe I would choke a little, but something always came up. I often wouldn't just get myself in trouble either; everyone else would suffer, too. A sock could lie in the middle of the living room floor and my mother would scream about this for 30 minutes; this is the mother I grew up with. I was a young girl and there were some things I just wasn't going to understand, but at a certain age the wisdom comes rushing in like a flood and all I can do is love the woman that kept me alive.

Runaway

For me, the trick is to run away before he does. I have never been the one to overstay my welcome in any man's heart because my fear of abandonment has robbed me from that. I told myself to never talk to desperation because I'll find myself happily waiting in an empty red room with throbbing walls, no furniture or décor, just a dying promise: a promise that declares the man I had fallen in love with simply "stepped out." As I wait and smile, smile and wait, the desperate voice continues, "Not to worry dear, I'm sure he'll be back any minute now." Pause. Desperation and I pass awkward glances at each other, occasionally stretching our lips into a distorted smile and I think *any minute now*...as I spend the reminder of my lifetime shamelessly switching my eyes back and forth between the clock that doesn't die and a door that doesn't open. I wait, rocking in my chair gleefully as the wooden floor screams. The eyes from inside picture frames freeze, looking at me like I'm artistically challenged. Only I would be able to see right through their pity for me. I would just ignore it, but that's what happens when every part of you decides it's love. A great big white flash explodes and abruptly I awake. I realize while I was sleeping in love, I denounced every piece of decency and integrity I owned. I stood in the center of a room barenaked, unarmed, and covered in paper-thin flesh. I could feel the cracks crawling on my face. My only excuse would be that I did it for love, but I'd rather spend my life running with wild horses chasing after the sun than running after a man that's chasing his escape from me.

Diamonds Are Forever

Somewhere in past lives, against the varied greys and future lives of electric blues, yet existing in truth within each and every dream, I remember searching for you. I remember scraping for you with my bare hands until the blood from my knuckles and fingernails, rushing out and exhausted, rested on the top of my skin, dried up, dying to get a peek of you. I remember digging with disheveled hair and a single shovel across corrupted lands where landmines used to be. I was in Sierra Leone, following a scent I knew, the scent I knew to be you. How is it that I knew you before I knew you? The secrets of my reincarnated souls whispered your cologne from unrecorded times just so I could find a resolution to my unresolved emptiness. Far too many times, I have followed what I didn't know in reverence to what is bigger than me. I searched through and through; I was looking for a diamond in a coalmine. Finally you came to me and I was in the form of an 18-year-old naïve girl who walked blindly and without certainty that I was placing each footstep on solid ground. I walked with difficulty, surviving and hopeful still that someone would be there to catch me if I fell. One day before I could crash into the ground like I usually do, your eyes held me and pulled me from gravity's crown. I hid behind your shadow from then on for protection like it was made of dark steel, forgetting that your shadows had shadows. Who was going to protect *you*? I took every single ounce of hope I had in man and placed it on your shoulders. I stacked it so high that it would potentially crush us both if you collapsed, and I held you responsible if you failed me. I remember I linked you to Jesus when I observed you passing by in white cloth and eating a loaf of bread. Your smile changed attitudes and your eyes compassioned a room; you were the one I've been looking for all this time...until you weren't. In my heart, I wanted to believe we disrupted a balance and the heavens roared in anger over our friendship, banishing our meaning to each other immediately. It was so unnaturally fast and unapologetic the way we disappeared from each other, like it was never supposed to happen in the first place. I would rather blame fate, the universe, the supernatural, anything, than look at the sadistic eyes of reality where I see your face and realize you had only turned into the kind of man I believed you were the only one incapable of being.

Poison

Poison, resembling the features of sadness but with more malice, crept its way inside of me, transforming my veins into black magic. Rooted in the depths of my soul: a pentacle, sword, wand, and chalice. I am powered by the spirit world as I feel it cling to me with a tight grip and daggered nails that dig at me for freedom. I had such reckless joy and a vibrant light, which so easily seeped out from the cracks of my skin, but now it dims a little more every day. I'm haunted by my hollow innards that remain settled and uninspired. My eyes are ink shot from want and all I have to show for it are my black tears. I try to write for the cure as I gather the frog legs, strands of hair, and wild spices to conjure up a victory of words because, without them, I'm sure to die.

Dreams

I look at the pictures of my imagination hanging perfectly on the walls of my crooked reality. I can't help but think these beautiful pictures just don't fit along such harsh wooden edges, and quietly my fears sat with me in agreement. I extracted their glory like a ripe fruit from the tree of my knowledgeable mind, believing that if I bit into it, I could bring them to life. In time, I began to notice the pictures had defiled themselves, mutilated and melted; the images could no longer fit within their designs in order to exist in a world I do not own, and it wasn't much longer until I noticed the contents in each picture started haunting me like Edvard Munch's "The Scream." There was an awful ooze coming out of the picture frames and I could hear them screaming in horror. I watched most of them fall to their colorful deaths, splashing beauty and pain, and the ones that survived crawled like desperate visions seeking one last chance at becoming real. But every one of them died before me. I watched with a hand to save them but I refused to touch them knowing I was unsure if I could keep them alive. *I don't know how to do this*, I think to myself. I don't know how to combine two distinct worlds.

So when no one else is looking, I run as far as I possibly can from the stagnant stills of my own truth and roam the unending busyness of my even greater and beautifully executed fictions written in my head. I come only as a quiet observer; looking for the perfect empty theatre seat, watching the life of my vast, immeasurable, and unobtainable dreams. Some days I have nowhere else to go but into the dimly lit fantasy that gives meaning to my possibilities. I worry as I glare at the infinite silver screen portraying me in countless futures that are just cartoons. It's hard for me to take them seriously, though God reassures me the idea of prophecies and purpose, the inner workings of work undone until it is. But in the meantime he tells me, "Wait for beauty; everything is beautiful in its time."

Inevitable

I'm not one to linger with inevitably. If the end, menacing as it as, decides it must lurk behind me with a raised collar and low brim hat in alley ways and street corners to catch me in some sort of demise, well, there will be no need. I will honor my fate and come toe to toe with tragedy. There will be no haunting scream or messy chase scene where I trip and fall, crawling backward on my hands and feet, pleading with the last to save me from stopping. No. My pride will not allow me to beg for what I have no control over. If the end has come, then let me be forward with the end in our meeting. "Do what it is that needs to be done and swallow me up in truth so that we can finally reach a peaceful union." Leave the haunting at the doorstep of the unresolved but be quick with me and my mortal eyes. If I was young, maybe I would run and never stop until my legs were plucked from me one by one, but more than ever I am tired now. I have been in constant warfare with this life as it is relentless with its tests and obstacles that age the body more than time. We endure constant blows like huge waves in the way we suffer, which can begin as early as the day we are born. Why would I begin another with inevitability? Of course I am sensible enough to know that if there was a fight between the two, I would lose.

Earth

The Earth's firstborns, green, lush, and bound to its soiled tongue, all rise up, exchanging slanted glances at one another, waiting for me to join the windy revolution. The bark, strong and silently judgmental, keeps his ranging opinions to himself, with no desire to express the paths I should take or the journeys I should go on. Instead, its nearly immortal body, occasionally decaying but always sturdy, stands watch like a guard at the gates of heaven. But everything else that is green and colorful, flexible and loose, urges me to go in the direction it is straining toward. Plants are always so hopeful, the Earth's endless descendants, cheering on the doomed, celebrating the enduring heart while praying for water for their own. No matter how much we destroy them and tread roughly on top of them, beneath us they smile, blowing wildly, helping us on our way.

Legs

I'm exhausted, only to find out I've been running, running in the exact same place. I'm bending, flexing, stretching, relaxing my muscles to make them care when I don't. I'm not in the mood to go to any lengths or travel to any distances, especially when my complacency demands a certain safety. Maybe it's the thought of progression that brings a sudden pain to my knees. Progress is an upward course. There is no turning back—just a sharp slanted slop that doesn't lend a ledge to the tired foot. So if forward is the only direction I must go, then a new heart must follow because the old one could not survive the higher altitudes. It would slowly worsen, unable to withstand the forgiving winds.

Rejection

My fears get the best of me. I fear too often, no one but man. There is something about his ambition when it defies righteousness that unsettles my soul, and I'm scared in a way I've never been before. I know never to get in the way of a man and his wants because, if necessary, he will leave a trail of dead bodies behind. Look closely at them as they lay twisted on the ground; there is a gaping hole in the center of their chests, where man, in his splendor, ripped every heart out in acknowledgement of his unruliness. I heed with caution and approach man like I would approach a wild stallion. I walk slow and steady; I'm trying to define his eyes. I see beauty and intellect, the wisdom in his soulful eyes, but naturally a man is untamed and wild at the touch. From a distance, my faith is confident and I approach him with probability, but up close his disturbingly still posture is intimidating because I can tell, with him, death is always a possibility. There is nothing left in him but power and strength; compassion is always the peaceful uncertainty. I thought maybe somewhere residing in the depth of my eye was the remedy that could rid the malice that clings to the heart of a man, but when he looks at me, I am just another victim. I'm brought to my knees by my inability to show man his humanity. I wanted so badly to possess the miracle to save the hopeful savage, the blessed monster. In my tears I am the sole reflection of the girl I can save. I look at man and wonder, "How can you love me if I can't save you?" "How can you save me if I can't love you?"

Writer

I smile at tragedies. I overanalyze corruption, and I hesitate at the sight of my own happy ending. I am a writer. There are moments when I see my happiness searching for me with the sort of joy that can move mountains of weary like a weightless seed, and somewhere the sky is ripping apart, piercing a godly light from heavenly boundaries just to observe the divinity. My happiness continually seeks me out, standing before me with a grin and an epiphany. I refer to our unions as déjà vu, like a dream that never happened. But I receive its presence as hope, though I never accept its invitation. I am young and the night is even younger. Happiness, I have never seen arms so open or hands so outstretched, pulling for me with an effort that must be love. As much as I want to be a part of that broken dawn, I only pretend I'm disgusted by it because it lacks a certain readership. Its perfection would only be a betrayal to me because, once it's all over, what will I do? Who will I be but a wordless delight? I would disappear in the scheme of things and I have so much more to offer than that. I publicly denounce all that resolves and question if the shadows will still come for me. The thunder draws me in, rolling in deep and thick, anticipating swallowing me whole. I obsess over the darkened greys and pitch black nights, the shocks of loud light hoping they will drag their sorrow out into a tangled web of bitter mess that I will write countless pages about. I'd rather be happy with sadness as I pull out my paper and pen and fill all the pages with pain. This reassures me the reason for my existence is not in vain.

Hero

I never wanted anything but to save you. Where do I have to go to reach the center of all evil and regain the souls of the innocent who have been held accountable for the sins they do not own? Who has put the pure up for ransom for momentary power and wealth? Already in ashes, they sit as a pile of dust and no one will ever remember their names or their unwilling sacrifice. So many suffer, wrenching and turning in the sea of burning flames and the taste of fire still caught in their mouth so we can't hear their screams. A multitude of souls caught between the crossfire of good and evil; some make it and some don't. It's hard to watch the people closest to me become victims and there's nothing I can do but chase after a cure I hope exists. Will my brother ever read my book? Can he muster up the bits and pieces of faith scattered inside his abandoned flesh and fight back against the malfunction that's shut him down to life? Can you even see what that looks like or recognize it? Sometimes I think if the opportunity arises and I came face to face with the thing that devours with unholy authority, I would martyr my own heart to emancipate the lost, the unlived, the untried, and give them their second chance at love and at peace. Because I've had these things whether for moment or a lifetime, and everyone deserves to know them.

The Fall

I've been falling for some time now. My panic goes in and out as I ponder whether I want to die smiling or die crying. I eventually laugh it all away as I watch the clouds transform from scene to scene, performing various episodes of my past life worth living. Anyway, the wind's meddling around my sensitive skin again, tickling my neck at first and then underneath my arms until I laugh, loudly listening to its musing stories from around the world. Whistling with promiscuity, the wind found tossing women's skirts up in front of men particularly entertaining. The men of course watched with a boggled excitement and sudden victory that nature, too, had a humorous side. But the beguiling ones were the people without much, who were simply waiting for a sign or a miracle. The ones waiting to be filled with faith and the wind would come to them, rushing in, cleansing the doubtful mind into a hopeful one. Every closed eye embarked on the rebirth of a new awakening. Every eyelash flickered with the last remnants of smoky dust from ashes past. "What a sight to behold," the wind whispered, "Every eye opening to the same world but seeing it differently." I reveled in the vision as the epiphany replayed in my life many times. "Far too often," I said, "you did this to me."

Death

I hope you are more than just the blackness they say you are. Some people speak of you as if they've seen you before. Somewhere in the darkness but further, where that black has not yet been defined, they say you sit in a chair made of unclean bones and wear a crown of rotted teeth and underneath your feet is a sea of endless corpses. The wickedness you are surrounded in, is it a rumor? Is your reign malicious or simply impartial? As a fraternal twin to life but always viewed as the less fond of the two, your likeness is by very few and only sought out if life comes across too cruel. Who is your employer, God or the devil? It's very much more likely you work for both, but doesn't it get to you, plucking one by one a life like cherries from a fruitful tree or petals from an abounding rose or a thorn from an unwanted weed? Do you feel sweet or sore about it? Is your heart made out of oil or wine, of saccharine or sickly-sweet? I think of you and I fear you, but I wonder if I can blame you for what must be certain.

Chains

I am draped in chains like a privileged slave, presenting this heavy metal as a sign of my oppression. And though it hides my flaws, it flatters my ignorance even more. I spin and twirl, parading my burdens like purple and prestige. I dance to prepare for the rain and pray it will wash away the memories I'm bound to and the ones I'm hopelessly devoted to. The small gaps in each link cling on to me in their first attempts to ambush my skin, peeling away at the layers of my self-consciousness until I'm raw and ready for the devouring. That look in my eye, the look of pain and pleasure, is from the shackle's claws that strangle my neck and wrists. I'm looking for the blood to spew out of me and, perhaps mixed with it, the contents of my freedom.

About the Author

Sharday Cage graduated from Saint Xavier University with a degree in Mass Communications. She currently resides in Chicago, Illinois, where she continues to pursue her passion as an up-and-coming writer and poet.

She began reciting her poetry at Saint Xavier, whereat she reached a pivotal moment: reciting her poem "Forgiveness" to Sister Helen Prejean, who has become a leading American advocate for the abolition of the death penalty and who was played by Susan Sarandon in the film based on her life, *Dead Man Walking*.

Sharday has since taken part in plays around the Chicago area, such as *Tomorrow Never Came*, about the innocent lives lost to gun violence, and *As You Are*, an inspirational play. Sharday's poetry has appeared in Record Magazine, an online poetry magazine that is dedicated to showcasing young poets, and at The Third City (thethirdcity.org).

Her previous poetry collection *Death of a Black Star*, which was released in 2011 by Sakura Publishing, has gained much popular attention and success. This poetry volume ranked on Amazon.com's Bestsellers List for African Poetry in both paperback and Kindle editions.

About the Artist

The Last Baroness, by Desislav Iliev (Courtesy of DexVision.com)

Desislav Iliev grew up in Bulgaria. His father and grandfather were both artists. He went to college for Iconography (Christian Icons Painting) and came to the U.S. in the summer of 2006. He then became a graphic and web designer, keeping painting and photography as hobbies. He lives in Chicago, Illinois.

www.ingramcontent.com/pod-product-compliance
Lightning Source LLC
Chambersburg PA
CBHW060948050426
42337CB00052B/2521